M000105542

CHOOSING A

LIFE PARTNER

by

Esther F. Akinladenu

Dedication

This book is dedicated to the Lord Jesus Christ, my redeemer and Savior. The only one that was crucified, shed His blood, died for my sins and rose again. He is alive forever! He gave me hope and the assurance of everlasting life, when I completely surrendered to Him.

In Him I live, and move, and have my being. He is the author and the finisher of my faith, the glory and the lifter of my head. He is my present help in time of need. He is highly exalted and given a name that is above all names.

I give all glory, honor and adoration to the King of kings and Lord of lords - the Alpha and Omega, the beginning and the end. He is the One who was, who is and who is to come. *"JESUS CHRIST THE SAME YESTERDAY, TODAY AND FOREVER."* - (Hebrews 13:8)

Acknowledgements

To God be all the glory, honor and adoration in Jesus name, for the grace to write this book. I believe it's the right, the perfect and God's appointed time. His word is true, powerful and forever settled.

"He has made everything beautiful at His time..." (Ecclesiastes 3:11).

I acknowledge the power, the presence and the manifestation of the Holy Spirit for the inspiration through which this book was written. It is a fact that the baptism of the Holy Ghost is a very precious and wonderful experience that every Christian needs in order to live a successful life. We need the power of God to effectively carry out divine assignments, for the fulfillment of His plans and purposes here on the earth.

I learnt a lot over the years from what my parents deposited in me. Thanks be to God for making my father and my mother, channels that brought me to this world and showered love and care on me -

the late Chief John O. Akindolire and late Chief Rachel O. Akindolire who are both forever in my memory.

To all my co-ministers, that supported me with prayers and words of encouragement before and during the writing of this book, I say "Thank you very much." I cannot mention everyone by name, but I pray that God will greatly reward your labor of love.

It is very important to show appreciation to Prophet David Gardiner (USA), who strongly spoke to me in his prophetic service, that it was time for me to "Start writing the books deposited into my heart by God." This powerful prophecy has now been confirmed.

My sincere gratitude goes to Evangelist Sharron Wesberry, who also prophesied under the Unction of the Holy Spirit, in some of her Prophetic services held in Dallas Texas. Thanks to my mentors; first of all my father in the Lord, Rev. Gabriel Farombi, the former General Overseer of Foursquare Gospel Church, Nigeria and the Founder/President of Refreshing Ministry world-wide. He is always there to guide, mentor and pray for me.

My appreciation also goes to Rev. Raphael Akinsulire, the vessel that God used to disciple and nurture me in my growing up years as a believer. I thank Rev Cornelius Adewale and my dear friend, Rev (Dr.) Oluyinka Osadare for their Godly counseling and prayers.

To all my brothers and sisters in Christ, I say "Thank you" for the role you played towards the successful completion of this book. As people begin to read it and get solution to their situations, so will God in the same measure bless you all abundantly, in Jesus name.

I appreciate Sister Elizabeth Hagan Asamoah, Astar Barkat, and Aisha Mafor Ndaloma for the significant role they played towards the successful outcome of this book. God bless you all. I also wish to thank Sister Joy Ntibundu, the editor of this book.

My special gratitude goes to my dear husband Pastor Ebenezer Akinladenu, for his prayers, encouragement and support in various ways that really motivated me to successfully complete this book. I also wish to really appreciate my beloved children for being there for me, and especially assisting me in the area of the use of technology to accomplish this divine assignment. You are all blessed, in the name of Jesus Christ

INTRODUCTION

This book is specially written with great passion, for the singles, and it is highly recommended that everyone yet to marry should read it for guidance before making the lifelong, final decision or commitment to a partner in marriage (whether already in a relationship or not yet). It's also good for those that are still single after separation from marriage, to discover the root-cause of the problems and mistakes they made in their first marriage, in order to make the necessary corrections.

Parents should also get this book for their teenagers before they are exposed to the inappropriate system of choosing life partners. This book is also recommended for married couples to help them trace the source of misunderstandings and lack of complete peace that hinder the full enjoyment of their marriage. As the content of this book is carefully read, understood, and put to practice there would surely be a solution.

The Lord removed every barrier, and opened the door of mercy to me in order to pour out what He had deposited in me for a life changing, warning, correction and direction to people who are in the process, or are yet to choose life partners. The scripture, Isaiah 45:2 is fulfilled as you hold a copy of this book in your hands.

"I will go before you and make the crooked places straight: I will break in pieces the gates of brass and put in sunder the bars of iron"

The instruction to write this book came with urgency, and this was in order to prevent people from going through the issue of falling into the same wrong pattern of choosing life partners. It is really an important life changing experience, and the proper application of the revealed information presented in this book, matters. With a full array of experiences drawn from personal, close relatives, individuals, group counseling, counseling of singles, couples, observations, and conference ministrations, the grace to write this book was made available. In addition, the inspiration through divine revelations, backed up with scriptures moved me to action, and the voice kept emphasizing to me that: **Choosing a life partner is the most important decision in life, therefore it** must be rightly, carefully, patiently and prayerfully handled. It is the foundation that marriage is built on. Life after marriage depends on the strength of the choice of a particular life partner. This is a choice that must be solidly made with strong material for the longevity of the marriage.

Unfortunately, however, a lot of people are falling into the trap of ignorantly making wrong choices on a daily basis. For example, some have lost their lives; and some are in dangerous and confused states. In order to remedy the situation, this book had to be written quickly to put in the hands of that individual or group that yearns for solution.

It takes an experienced driver that has been through a road with different features like deep pot holes, sharp corners, dangerous bends, bridges, rough and some smooth areas to have the true picture and full description of that road. The experienced driver should be able to *alert* intending drivers that have never passed through that road before about the true condition of the road. It's only a wicked and selfish driver that will hold back from alerting other drivers about the danger and condition of the road they are about to travel on.

After thoroughly reading this book, you will be able to understand that "**Choosing a Life Partner**" will determine the pattern of your life, either to succeed and fulfill your destiny, or fail and make a shipwreck of your destiny depending on your choice. I believe that this book will help and guide you to choose the right life partner with true love through God's guidance according to His will. It will also bring preventive measure to the present generation from going through the wrong route caused by ignorance and lack of necessary information.

It is very important for the intending "drivers" to listen attentively, obey the instructions of an experienced "driver" in order to avert the dangers and problems on the road and enjoy a safe and successful journey. The good news is that the obedient ones would easily pass through the road and enjoy their trip to the fullest. Unfortunately, however, the disobedient and stubborn ones may have a rough and turbulent journey, that is, if they happen to survive it.

"If you are willing and obedient, you will eat the good fruits of the land" - (Isaiah 1:19).

"He that have ears to hear, let him hear..." - (Mathew 11:15).

This book is a "balanced diet," rich enough to guide intending persons through the unknown journey of choosing life partners. Also for those who are already in relationships or in courtships, you will understand how to take off, know the expected road signs on the way, be aware of safety precautions and identify tips for a safe and successful journey. It's like a Global Positioning System (GPS), that will guide you to make the right and wise decisions according to God's will.

Marriage is a journey. Yes, a journey of a lifetime, and therefore a solid preparation must be made to choose the right passenger that will ride with you throughout this journey. Beyond any doubt, it is a fact that the major cause of problems in the society is *CHOOSING THE WRONG LIFE PARTNER*.

You will see a lot of the factors to take into consideration as you read this book. I encourage you to read every chapter, study, and meditate on it, and then apply it to your situation. Somebody you will live with for the rest of your life should be carefully and prayerfully chosen: "**Prevention is better than cure.**"

To the married couples who have prayerfully and patiently chosen life partners, and their union is proving to be successful and are enjoying happy married life, I say "A big congratulations to you!" The Lord will continue to uphold your home and bless your family. To those who have ignorantly started the journey, especially before salvation, and found obstacles and lots of mountains on the way; the Lord will restore your marriage and give you a new or fresh start in life in Jesus name. The mercy of God will prevail, and all shall be well as you call upon Jesus for help and divine intervention.

"The righteous cry, and the Lord heareth, and delivereth them out of all their destructions" (Ps 34:17)

"The time of ignorance therefore God over-looked...." (Acts 17:30)

You just need to appreciate the unconditional love of God towards you and surrender yourself to His will and ways because *".....God is love"* (1 John 4:8)
The first step in the journey is to be a child of God, therefore *"...as many as received him, to them gave He power to become the sons of God..."* (John 1:12). Whatever category you may belong now, whether you are already in a relationship, not there yet, at the verge of making a choice or you have already chosen a life partner, I strongly believe that you will find a lot of helpful

information in this book to guide you before you finally say "I do" because knowledge is power.

CHAPTER 1
Who is a Life Partner?

A life partner is somebody you choose to spend the rest of your life with as a spouse. When you choose a particular person as your future spouse and eventually get married, both of you will live together forever as life partners. That decision automatically makes both of you to become companions for life, and from then on both of you will begin to bear the same name, live under the same roof, bear children, acquire same properties and do everything together in common.

Marriage was instituted by God, and it is a covenant entered into between a man and a woman, just as it was for Adam and Eve. God is interested in marriage to the point in which He declared in Genesis 2:18 that: "......*It is not good for a man to be alone. I will make him a help meet...*"

It is therefore very important to involve God in choosing the right person, because He is the originator and founder; the giver of perfect gift.

There is a right woman for every man and a right man for every woman. He gave Eve to Adam, just in the same way He would give you your spouse. Even though they both fell, yet the unconditional love of God brought redemption and reconciliation through the Lord Jesus Christ. *God is always available to guide and protect the partners chosen according to His will.* They will always survive storms and obstacles, and be victorious in their life journey, no matter how tough.

Choosing a life partner is the most important decision a human being can make to determine the fulfillment of his or her destiny. Your life revolves around the person you choose to be your spouse, and for that reason your choice can build you or destroy you; it can bring total victory to your destiny or bring complete ruin. The life and success of your children depends on your choice of life partner. Your career and ambition can come to reality and be successfully delivered, or become aborted, resulting in a failed project, depending on the choice you make. Who are you planning to choose? STOP!

"And you shall know the truth and the truth shall make you free."- (John 8:32).

Your chosen life partner can contribute to your success in life and can also bring failure and despair to your life. He or she can assist you to reach your goal and attain your glorious destiny or destroy it. Whoever you choose as your life partner will determine the pattern of the rest of your life from the day you make a final decision to live with this person. Because your choice can strengthen or break you, it is very important to be careful, prayerful, watchful, and be patient before you choose.

The choice of a life partner is something you cannot renounce. In order to deal with the danger of wrong choice in marriage, be very careful and be sure of whom you choose. Remember that this is the person you are going to spend the rest of your life with, you must therefore know this person spiritually, physically, socially, financially, morally, and intellectually. Below are the possible questions you may need to ask before you make your decision.

Possible Questions You Need To Ask Yourself

1. Is this person God fearing and obedient to God's words? *"Whosoever fears the LORD has a secure fortress, and for their children it will be a refuge."*(Proverbs 14:26)

17

2.   Can you see faithfulness and honesty in him or her?

3.   Is your life partner someone that corrects when necessary, and honest enough to speak the truth in love without flattery? This is because: *"**Open rebuke is better than secret love. Faithful are the wounds of a friend; but the kisses of an enemy are deceitful**"* - (Proverbs 27:5-6 KJV).
*"**A man who flatters his neighbor Spreads a net for his feet**"* - (Proverbs 29:5 NKJV).

4.   Is this person the type that offers wise counsel?

5.   Do you know the level of this person's temperament? *It is not wise to choose somebody with serious hot temper.* If you cannot succeed in dealing with it during relationship, know that it will only get worse after marriage. If you are not comfortable with it, don't manage it. *Do not endanger your future in the name of love that will not last.* The Bible clearly warns us in Proverbs 22:24-25, not to befriend an angry man in order not to learn his ways and be ensnared:

"Make no friendship with an angry man; and with a furious man thou shalt not go. Lest thou learn his ways, and get a snare to your soul."

6.   Does this person have control over his/her appetite?

7.   How compassionate is your future spouse?

8.   Is he or she a positive thinker? *"A merry heart doeth good like a medicine: but a broken spirit drieth the bones."* - (Proverbs 17:22).

9.   Is the person you want to choose hardworking or lazy?

10.   How generous or stingy is he or she?

11.   Is he or she prayerful?

12.   How often does your partner read the bible? Remember what the Bible declares to us in Joshua 1:8: *"This book of the law shall not depart out of thy mouth; but thou shalt meditate therein day and night, that thou mayest observe to do according*

to all that is written therein: for then thou shalt make thy way prosperous, and then thou shalt have good success."

13. What is the level of this person's Christian life and commitment to the service of God?

14. Is he or she really sincere and serious about the relationship?

15. What legal issues do your partner have? *Note that you are, (or going to be) part of everything in his or her life, past present and future.*

16. Do you know the level of his or her education?

17. Are you sure of his or her true marital status and background, and are you satisfied with it?

18. Does he or she already have a child or children with somebody else, if so, are you duly informed about it?

19. Who are his or her friends? "**Show me your friend and I will tell you who you are.**" This

is not just a random quote from nowhere, it is a Bible concept from King Solomon and it is found in Proverbs 13:20: *"He that walketh with wise men shall be wise: but a companion of fools shall be destroyed."*

20. What can you say about his or her social life? Is he or she addicted to anything? For example: smoking, alcohol, partying, etc. Are you okay with that? It's better to end a relationship if you can't cope with some habits than to start a big fight after marriage. The best option is to use your love influence in helping him/her quit, and get out of every addiction completely before commitment.

21. Does he or she tell the truth or lie a lot?

22. Can you see your partner as forgiving and willing to admit when he or she is wrong?

23. How humble is he/she?

24. Does this person respect confidentiality?

25.   Are you comfortable with the appearance and look - the height, weight, facial and other features, or are you just trying to tolerate him/her for a personal reason? This could cause a very serious problem in future after making a choice and you begin to look out there for someone more attractive.

You need to be very satisfied with the appearance of your life partner. Remember also that you cannot base your choice on physical attractions. Consider first the inward beauty, which is the character of a person. Some are beautiful outside and inside, while some others are good looking outside and terribly bad inwardly. While some are not physically attractive, they are very excellent inwardly.

Whatever the case may be, remember that we are all created in the image of God. The above are just some of the questions you need to ask yourself, and they are meant to be a guide to help you to identify who really a true and genuine life partner is. There are so many other factors that should be taken into consideration for proof depending on individual situation. It is very important to be watchful and be vigilant before making a choice. **According to the principle of God, confirmed in** the bible, a male Christian should choose a female partner and settle together as husband and wife. A Christian who is truly born again must follow God's principle in all areas of life, including choosing a life partner.

"Then the rib which the LORD God had taken from man He made into a woman, and He brought her to the man. ....Therefore a man shall leave his father and mother, and be joined to his wife, and they shall become one flesh." (Genesis 2:22, 24 (NKJV)).

"And he answered and said unto them, Have ye not read, that he which made them at the beginning made them male and female, And said, For this cause shall a man leave father and mother, and shall cleave to his wife: and they twain shall be one flesh? " (Mathew 19:4-5)

Above all, **PRAY** and be sure that you are choosing the right person that you will peacefully and successfully spend the rest of your life with. God bless you.

CHAPTER 2
The Appropriate Time

There is time for everything in the life of human beings. As a Christian there is an appointed time to choose a life partner who you will later get married to.

"To everything there is a season and a time to every purpose under the heaven..." - (Ecclesiastes 3:1).

It is real that the ultimate end product of choosing a life partner is marriage. This largely depends on a successful courtship. *Marriage is instituted for men and women and not for boys and girls. Maturity is therefore required for readiness in making the choice of a life partner.* You need to know and understand exactly what you want and what you are doing.
A lot of the problems in marriage today are due to boys and girls ignorantly getting married without the knowledge of what marriage really is all about. What they call love is actually lust, and it is

not a wise decision for a teenager to go into marriage. Although maturity levels may vary, yet age has a huge role to play when it comes to choosing a life partner. Your youthful age is the best time to be in active service for the kingdom of God. Why don't you enjoy your youthful age as a single, working and doing a lot of exploits for the Lord before getting into the responsibility of marriage; children and matrimonial issues?

Marriage is a life long journey therefore don't rush into it. *"Rushing in, produces a rushing out."* **Meanwhile, the suggested age range for choosing a life partner is between the ages of twenty-one to twenty-nine years old.** Not too early and not too late. It should be within young adult age level. Refusing to choose a life partner at the right time may cause long time delay. This is more common with ladies. Being too picky, arrogant or being proud can make you lose the right person. Some men want to stay longer as singles to avoid heading the family responsibilities, and settling down with one woman. This is not a good option.

Likewise, some ladies delay becoming wives because they don't see themselves capable of submitting to a man as the head of the home. This is a dangerous game that can cause permanent singleness. There is time for everything. A mature individual can resist temptations, make wise decisions, control emotions, maintain self restraint or discipline and be more stable than a teenager.

Apart from age and maturity, it is very necessary and important to be educationally, vocationally and financially stable before making final commitment to a life partner. Though the relationship may be in progress while in school, care must be taken to make sure that the eagerness to get married does not cause hindrance to your academic pursuit and progress in your career. It may not be easy to continue to pursue your education after you have tied the knot. Be wise, and plan ahead to be an achiever.

The fact that you have reached the suggested or appropriate age for marriage does not mean you should rush into a relationship. Rushing headlong into a relationship with desperate scheming in mind is a dangerous venture that never ends well. Motivated by anxiety, you don't need to stress yourself out by deliberately dressing inappropriately, buying expensive materials beyond your budget, wearing excessive makeup, and showing off in order to gain attention of the opposite sex. These are not at all necessary. Try as much as possible to follow the following guidelines:

- Make sure you keep yourself clean and neat. Personal hygiene is very important - your entire body from head to toe must be clean. Your hair should be well taken care of (especially ladies). Appropriate hair style for ladies and men is necessary. God has given you the right and the best hair color, you don't need to change it to outrageous colors. Something as routine as daily shower and oral hygiene are very important. There are some things that seem insignificant but very important. Take good care of your body using good deodorants and lotions.

- Wear clean, simple and appropriate clothes. Don't make yourself vulnerable by exposing your valuable body, you are beautifully and wonderfully made. The glory of God is in you and your body is the temple of God.

- Prepare your mind with scriptures concerning your choice. Picture the person in your mind, and ask specifically from God like Hannah, who asked for a baby boy. She did not say "Just give me a child." Describe the type of person you want to live with for life and allow God to take control. Final decision belongs to Him. If you happen to get a confirmation of somebody different from your request, pray very well and let your pastor pray along with you too. God knows all things. Don't allow ignorance to lead you into rejecting or refusing someone that God has for you.

- Submit your will to God's will.

- Do not let your heart be troubled and your mind disturbed concerning choosing a life partner. You can relax and allow the Holy Spirit to guide and direct you. Release your heart for the move of the Holy Spirit. Allow the Spirit of God to flow out of your belly like river you will experience the joy and peace of God.

- Do not be anxious. Be cool, calm, and patient. *"Be anxious for nothing, but in everything by prayer and supplication with thanksgiving let your request be made known to God"* (Philippians 4:6).

- Talk to God in prayer for guidance and *DIVINE CONNECTION* to the right person.

- Pray for discerning spirit to be sure you are making the right choice. It will be disastrous to choose a counterfeit instead of the original. Do not take Ishmael for Isaac.

- Get deeply involved in God's work at your church or the ministry assigned to you. Stay focused in God's service. You don't need to show off, advertise yourself or try to get attention. Let your motive for doing it be pure and not for self reward. God knows how to work it out for you.

- Attend young adults' fellowship and seminars regularly.

- Brother, please be sensitive to the Holy Spirit if He is leading you to talk to a lady. As long as you are sure of God's leading, don't be too proud to go to her if you happen to be richer or feel superior to her. On the other hand, don't feel inferior or unworthy to speak to her if she seems to be wealthier or in higher level than you in any area. Total obedience to the true voice and conviction from God is very important.

- Sister, please respond wisely and politely when approached by a suitor. Don't just say "yes" in desperation and anxiety. Don't say "no" hastily in order to make him feel that you are not desperate. Wait patiently in prayer, but don't deliberately delay after receiving the answer. The Spirit will bear witness. Be careful; don't say "no" when you mean or are supposed to say "yes" if you have peace and confidence about the decision.

- Brother, do not make up dreams or false revelations in order to gain the heart of a lady. If you are led by God's Spirit to talk to a lady and seek her consent in becoming your life partner, please tell her the truth and go straight to the point. If she is meant for you she will surely grant your request when the time is right.

- Do everything in moderation, including your speech.

- Trust in the Lord and be sensitive to God's instruction. "*For as many as are led by the Spirit of God, they are the sons of God.*" - (Romans 8:14).

- Let your focus be on a true child of God. Don't try to make just anybody your partner. Be connected with Christians. *"Do not be unequally yoked together with unbelievers. For what fellowship is righteousness with lawlessness and what communion has light with darkness?*"- (2 Corinthians 6: 14)

CHAPTER 3
Why Make The Choice?

The one salient reason for making the choice of a life partner must be based on God's will. The Spirit of God must bear witness within you that he/she is the right one for you. Genuine love must reflect in your choice. *Choose for love. Any other reason apart from the will of God with genuine and unconditional love is very wrong and will result in short lived relationship.*

A) Examine Your Motive
Ask yourself why do you want to choose that lady or that man as your life partner? Your choice should not be based on facial and physical appearance, e.g., He or she is "cute," handsome, beautiful, good looking, has smooth skin, tall, short, slim, big, strong muscles, hair shape, set of teeth, and other remarkable features that will make your decision surely short lived. If you are choosing him or her because of wealth or riches,

the relationship comes to a permanent dead end as soon as there is financial challenge.

A relationship with wrong motives can never last; choose with love. I John 4:8 reveals to us that:

*"**Whosoever does not love does not know God, because God is love.**"*

If you choose based on appearance (the way he or she looks), you should also keep in mind that physical changes do occur, either naturally or otherwise, because:

1) **Accidents or incidents**, such as car, fire etc, of any kind could happen to affect a particular part of the body you sincerely appreciate.

2) **Sickness** could happen in the family and change the appearance or ability of a spouse.

3) **Ageing**, there will be changes in facial and body appearance due to age.

4) **Skin diseases**, like pimples, eczema etc can occur to affect changes in facial appearance.

5) **Hair color or style change** - gray hair, hair loss or certain type of hair cut can produce a different look. However, women have the advantage of covering their real hair with wigs.

6) **Decrease, increase or discontinuing of facial makeup**, - any of these reasons could cause a lot of changes in a person's appearance. Some people cover their real facial appearance with makeup, and it can become a big issue when the real facial appearance is revealed without makeup.

7) **Weight loss**, - there may be changes in appearance if he or she decides to lose weight intentionally. What of weight loss by an unintentional situation or through sickness?

8) **Weight gain**, - your partner may gain weight and look different.

9) **Loss of teeth**, - your partner may lose his or her teeth which may alter his or her look.

10) **Injury or deformity** of any part of the body, such as broken bones or paralysis may cause

disabilities or even put him or her on a wheel chair.

11) He or she **may lose one or both eyes** to sickness or accident, or for any other reason.

12) **Unexpected serious health issue** may occur that will alter normal body functions, and so many other things not mentioned here.

Once any or some of these things happen, a relationship that is based on appearance and facial looks is completely affected. Nobody expects these things, but what if they happen? Physical appearances are subject to change. True love should not be bothered or moved by any physical changes, but rather work and deal with it, because you have a soul mate for a partner. By faith, continue to admire and love the real person that you choose, regardless of the changes that may occur in the future, whether positive or negative.

Do you choose a partner because of riches? What if the money is no longer available? Remember, a poor man today may become a millionaire tomorrow. God is able to raise someone from a dunghill to a pinnacle, a good example is Joseph, a prisoner who became second in rank to the king of Egypt overnight.

God is so powerful; He can open a door, and can also shut it. He can remove anyone from a particular position at anytime. He can promote and lift anyone up as He pleases. He can also pull down as we see in the case of Queen Vashti, in the book of Esther chapter one. She was driven out of the palace from the position of a queen to nobody, in couple of minutes. **"No condition is permanent."**

It is not right to make a choice of life partner because of the gifts or talents a person possesses such as the ability to sing, dance, play instruments, or possess skills for oratory, sports, and games and so on. These things may stop for any reason at any time you least expect, then your purpose of relationship is defeated and problem steps in. Let God's leading guide you to the right direction and put you in the right hand. Allow Him to do it in His own way as you trust absolutely in Him. *True love should be a good reason for choosing a person that you will spend the rest of your life with.*

Don't be enticed by physical appearance and base your judgment totally on it. Don't get me wrong. It is important to choose someone who you are comfortable with the way he or she looks, yet, you should pray to have the assurance that you are making the choice according to God's will. **Remember that *you are choosing the real him or her and not just the looks and achievement.***

Relationship based on the will of God with genuine love will not be moved by any unexpected situation but will wax stronger even in the face of adversity. Some have simply chosen life partners based on the person's titles, fame, or popularity in sports, music, political offices, and business. Others include the person's recognized positions in the society, educational achievement, family affluence, travelling opportunity abroad and influence, wealth, power, etc. All these are good, but they should not be a foundation for a relationship.

The fact that the person goes to church and participates in church activities should not be considered as enough reason to make a life commitment. Some people go to church in order to seduce the children of God and lure them into wrong relationships. Beware and be warned.

Wait a minute! Did you pray enough and seek God's face before taking this important life decision? Did you inform the ministers and elders of your church before making the decision? Be watchful and be prayerful. Don't fall victim in the hands of agents of darkness. They are spoilers and glorious destiny destroyers of young and naive Christians, especially young adults with great calling of God over their lives. The goal of such deceivers is to stop them from carrying out their present and future assignments. They appear in sheep's clothing but they are wolves among the sheep.

"The thief comes not but to steal, kill and destroy, but I have come to give you life and give you more abundantly." - (John 10:10).

"Submit yourselves therefore to God. Resist the devil and he will flee from you"-   James 4:7.

The thoughts and plans of God towards you are thoughts of peace and not of evil, to give you an expected end. Stay in His will; operate under His power and anointing to be an overcomer and a victor.

B) Is Love Really Blind?
A lot of people say that "**Love is blind.**" This is not true at all. It's just a self justification for choosing according to their feelings and will, therefore pretending to be blind to already known situation of the partner in order to achieve their selfish goal. Whoever does that and closes his or her eyes

to important aspects of a partner without properly addressing it with solution before making a choice, is **blind indeed, selfish and wicked.** The ones involved are simply doing what they want to do without following God's guidance. They decide to be deliberately blind. Entering into a relationship without an atom of love is foolishness. People that play this kind of game know deep down in their hearts that the relationship will not last.

Here is somebody that you know is addicted to some unacceptable ways of life, even towards you, yet you still went ahead to choose him or her because of your selfish motive. ***The most common one is the attraction to travel to the developed countries with the individual for financial success.***

- **Travel to Developed Countries**

Choosing a person in order to have the opportunity of joining him/her overseas is common among those who are desperately bent on achieving selfish ambitions without any iota of love. They close their eyes to the unacceptable, unbearable attitudes and issues that could negatively impact the person's life. Such people later come out in full color to use the attitudes as excuse to fight and separate after achieving their dream of travelling overseas, thereby exposing their partner to the public ridicule or shame instead of helping him or her to solve the problems. They act as if they were ignorant of the behavior of this partner before travelling to join him or her. I see this type of act as wickedness of the highest order, pure hatred and fake relationship, instead of genuine and true love.

The relationship may be a way of transforming the person's life if only the partner had given condition to the partner that the continuation of the relationship would depend on change of behavior before the choice and process of travelling could be made. How about fervent prayer and advice that could go a long way? *"Speaking the truth in love"* is a biblical fact and Godly way.

The problem becomes compounded as someone's heart is broken by early separation after the goal of travelling abroad is achieved. This is a serious, dangerous and deceitful act. Those that are involved in this kind of act need to ask for God's mercy with humility, and make restitution.

Are you a single individual that is planning to join a partner abroad? I strongly advise you to only do so with genuine love and not hidden agenda. It's not good to bite the finger that feeds you. Why will you agree to go with someone if the character and ways of life are not completely satisfactory to you? This is mostly common among ladies. Unfortunately, in some countries, women are given certain privileges and rights which some take advantage of. Some ladies use the advantages against their spouses that brought them abroad.

"Be not deceived. God is not mocked, for whatsoever a man soweth that shall he also reap" - (Galatians 6:7).

Let the fear of God be in you. Choose for love and according to God's will. It is a pity that some people are now choosing unknown individuals as life partners, especially from the internet and special arrangement. There are several examples of this type of issues, for example, there was a case, where a woman on wheel chair posted her photograph on a web dating page, only her beautiful face showed and she attracted a young man, who later processed her visa by all means to join him overseas. As soon as he sighted her, he collapsed as he saw a woman on wheel chair, and he was rushed to the hospital. The same woman with the same face who was supposed to be his life partner for immediate wedding.

Another instance is about a man who took a photograph with stethoscope and a medical uniform in front of a popular hospital in the USA and stole the heart of a beautiful lady by proving to her that he was a medical doctor. He succeeded in bringing the lady, from her country in Africa, in order to officially marry her abroad. This lady experienced the shocking moment of her life when she discovered that this man was a Nurse Aide; in a Nursing Home for Elderly people shortly after her arrival. There is nothing wrong in doing that job, but the idea of deceiving her with false identity is very wrong.

Regardless of your physical appearance, your career or financial status, there is somebody God has prepared to be your life partner. You don't need to describe yourself as a bank manager when you are a gate man at the bank. Stop deceiving people by hiding your identity. Remember there will be exposition when you least expect, the consequence will be very disastrous. Ladies and Gentlemen: make sure you really know who you're choosing before the final commitment. Do not start courtship after wedding, take note that marriage is not an experiment that you want to try and see if it would work out or not.

- **Desperation to have Children:**

Some people desperately make choices in haste, probably just to have children by all means, because in their minds their "Biological clock is ticking," and they only need an agreeable somebody to make it happen. This is not a proper foundation for a genuine relationship, because it is like a house built upon water, - it will collapse and fall apart in no time. Such people just needed biological children by sleeping with anybody through wedlock.

There was a story of a rich woman that travelled from a country in South Africa to another country in West Africa (her country), to find a man to marry for the sake of having children. She was introduced to a brother, who was about to get married in a couple of months to a devoted lady, a worker in the church, after about one and half years of courtship. This brother was enticed with the money, and quickly agreed to marry her within couple of days of their relationship. Immediately after the wedding, he ended up travelling with the woman to South Africa. He left a big wound in the heart of the lady chosen for him by God.

The other woman pretended to really love him; but unfortunately, it was just to achieve her goal and fulfillment of her desire of having children. She showered him with money and gifts. The man selfishly traveled with a strange woman to a strange place, for the love of money and not the genuine love for her. Entering into that strange woman's life brought a big disappointment to the innocent sister with true relationship and genuine love for him. He became blind internally, physically, and spiritually. The woman had a baby girl within one year for him, and there was fake happiness and deceptive good relationship. The second baby (boy) arrived a year and one month after the birth of the first baby. Mission was accomplished.

A few weeks later after the arrival of the second baby the man was driven out of her house unexpectedly and surprisingly, during a planned argument initiated by her. He went back to her country in West Africa empty handed and with shame. He was not allowed to take any of his clothes or other belongings. After all, she gave him everything and also took everything back from him. What a miserable life! Both of them made wrong choices for personal and selfish reasons. This is far from the will of God. Thanks be to God, the lady he left behind in West Africa with great disappointment, got married to a wonderful blessed man of God few months before his arrival. No wonder single parenthood is increasing in number on daily basis. ***The most common factor*** *for single parenthood is due to wrong choice of partner.* This mistake could occur either from a man or a woman who is desperate to have babies by all means. The interest and focus is based on the baby with the benefits attached to single parenthood (especially in advanced countries) and not in the success of the relationship. *"Love of money is the root of all evil."* The future and destiny of your children is more valuable than the undeserved money you are getting temporarily with greed and selfishness.

Remember, it is far better to raise children in a family with both the father and mother than with just a single parent. It can negatively affect mental, moral, intellectual and every aspect of a child's life. Choose for love; get married to the right one. Have babies according to the plan of God for marriage (procreation). Raise your children together in unity and peace.

- **Wedding Celebration and fun:**

Some people are quick to run into relationship and rush into marriage. Wedding ceremony involves big Party, eating, drinking, dancing, receiving gifts, music, social gathering, decorations, attractive wedding outfits, shopping, etc. It does not matter to them what follows after the ceremony; people tend to close their eyes to the meaning, purpose and importance of marriage as long as people gather to celebrate. They have celebrants' dance to show the ability to dance and to display all kinds of dance moves, with gorgeous attires and enjoyment of the moment.

They pretend not to pay attention to the issues and situations in their partner's life. This is very unacceptable. This is another terrible and wrong motive to marry. It's like a tree without roots. No wonder, I heard about a wedding that was based on this reason that was dissolved even before the photographer of the wedding ceremony brought the pictures. The husband abandoned the new bride within a couple of weeks after the wedding, because of a minor quarrel. The photographer was very disappointed as it was not easy for him to get the balance for his service. Quickly bills piled up from different services and the new marriage became strained to a breaking point!

Think deeply and realize that the crowd will leave, music will stop, and you will remove the wedding outfits; the celebration will surely be over. Then what is next? Wedding ceremony should never be a priority; life after the wedding should matter most. Good relationship with true love should continue after wedding ceremony.

Don't allow one day of celebration ruin your entire life and destiny.

- **Imitation/Competition**

In some cases, people think and say most of their close friends are married. Brothers, sisters, cousins, some close relatives Colleagues, co-workers, church members, neighbors etc are engaged; so they become desperate to get married as quickly as possible with any available opportunity of proposal. Therefore, anybody becomes the chosen one in order to hastily do what other people are doing. Stop! "Imitation is a bad disease." and it is dangerous. All fingers are not equal. There is time for everything. Wait for your time.

Open your eyes to see and spend quality of time in courtship before the final commitment of a life partner is made. Don't imitate those that rush in. The fact that some people are getting married around you does not mean you should do the same. "God's time is the best." Do not base your choice on imitation. Doing what others are doing and following other people's examples is not a right reason to choose a life partner hastily. Open your eyes and see if he or she is the right person for your life and feel true love with patience.

You may compete concerning dress codes, speech, cars, jobs etc., with your friends, family members or colleagues. Those things can fade away and be physically destroyed, and you can easily get another one. You can even return or exchange them. Those things can be given out or lent to people. However, be informed that you cannot exchange or trade your chosen life partner. It's a life choice, a very serious matter. Give it a deep thought and be very patient. You don't have to hastily choose just anybody in competition or imitation. Be original.

Pressure from Family
Another important factor for wrong choice of life partner is too much pressure from family members and friends. The choice is made anyway in order to satisfy them and make yourself look good before them. Be warned; the result may be very disastrous. There was a lady that went through this type of situation few years ago. She was pressured by some close family members into a relationship that finally ended in marriage against her wish. They told her she could easily get out after wedding if didn't like the marriage. **"Pencil marks can easily be erased using an eraser as they are both made by the same manufacturer,"** - they assured her.

Alas! The marriage did not last six months. The lady knew it was not going to last, but listened to the compelling statements and wrong advice. This was due to ignorance of the real meaning and purpose of marriage. The man was discovered to have been married to another woman with a child. She was deceived. What a great mistake! At last she was blamed and became an object of ridicule, especially by the family members who lured her to it. Her reason for choosing him was not based on personal conviction, and God's word, she being an unbeliever at that time who did not know the importance of the word of God and the power of prayers.

You still need to be patient and know who you are choosing as life partner despite the fact that you are under pressure. Remember, it's going to be you alone in the situation at the end of the day. Be wise. Learn from other people's mistakes.

Let your choice be pure, genuine and come from the heart. Don't let it be based on somebody's idea. A choice of life partner based on other people's persuasion and suggestion is going to end in disaster and failure. In some cases, there may be divine connection through family members or friends, yet you still need to make sure and know for yourself that he or she is the right one for you. Take the matter to God in prayer and watch closely to know the person you are to commit your life to. Other people's testimonials and approvals about somebody are not enough to convince you in choosing a life partner, so be very careful when you are in the process of making your choice. This is because when things do not work well, they will be the first to testify against you, and unfortunately, it may be too late.

CHAPTER 4
It's Okay To Say 'No'

You need to say "no" to immorality, **to sex before marriage**; and say "no" to anything that will make you compromise your faith in God. In a relationship with genuine love, it should not be much of a difficult thing for partners to agree to wait till wedding day before sleeping together. Beware of someone that pressurizes you persistently for sex before marriage. It's against God's will. As a true child of God, remember that **"Your body is the temple of God."** Such act is a willful sin against the Lord, and it's simply called fornication (sexual intercourse between people who are not married to each other). The Bible warns us in 1 Corinthians 6:18-19:

"Flee fornication. Every sin that a man practice is without the body but he that commit fornication sins against his own body. Do you know that your body is the temple of the Holy Spirit which you have from God? You are not your own."

Do not make yourself slave to immorality in order to secure a relationship. Don't sell your body in desperation for marriage, thinking that would hasten your partner's acceptance to marry you. Unfortunately, ninety percent (90%) of such relationships do not end in marriage. Very few ends up in "**Suffering in silence kind of marriage,**" because the foundation lacks honor and dignity. The situation is like *a beautifully wrapped gift item meant to be presented at an event, but it has its wrapping paper torn, thereby exposing it to public before it is presented to the intended recipient.*

Will such a gift still be valuable on the very day of the occasion? The beauty or suspense it ought to attract is gone, and it's no longer new or exciting. For this reason it's considered worthless and valueless. The whole purpose of wanting to present a beautiful, wrapped, and intact gift to intending recipient is defeated. What a pity!

A man or woman that tells you that he or she needs to see your body, and check out your sexual ability before making a decision of life partner with you, does not have genuine love for you. There is no trust, respect or seriousness in your relationship. The presence of love in any relationship compels partners to respect each other's dignity. The Epistles to the Corinthians in

Chapter 13:4-7 (NIV) clearly present to us the expression or attributes of true love.

"Love is patient, love is kind. It does not envy, it does not boast, it is not proud. It does not dishonor others, it is not self seeking, it is not easily angered, it keeps no record of wrongs. Love does not delight in evil but rejoices with the truth. It always protects, always trusts, always hopes, always perseveres"

Making a request may happen in few cases, yours is to say "NO!" Request may be made in various ways:

➤ **Physical Action**:
(Action speaks louder than words). If you are alone with your partner and you notice that he's beginning to make some moves that you feel are inappropriate, even without making a verbal request, you need to stop the action and say no to what is about to happen. You can wisely leave the scene and find your way out of trouble.

➤ **Verbal Request:**
Request can be verbally made in a subtle way, trying to use it as a sign of love and assurance of future marriage. It doesn't

matter how it is presented, the answer must be no.

➢ **Touching**:
Excessive or inappropriate touching of each other's body should be discouraged. There should be a limit to the touching of certain parts of the body that may cause uncontrollable emotional reaction. Stop before you unconsciously fall into lust instead of love.

➢ **Looking:**
When you see somebody looking at you lustfully, it is a strong sign of falling into premarital sex. It may be by winking, making facial or mouth signs, take your leave. Run from evil appearance before its manifestation.

➢ **Speech:**
Some people know how to make request through love speech. They flatter you and make a description of you with exaggeration. The sweet speech can stir you up to unconscious move into wrong action. Be wise and run from the appearances of evil. Quickly stop listening to such sweet talk.

> **Wrongly Quoting the Scriptures:**
  There are some passages of the Bible that people quote and interpret wrongly in order to deceive. They deliberately do this to suit their immoral intentions or acts. The truth and fact is that sex is absolute for husband and wife. So, save it till your wedding day.

> **Giving Inappropriate Examples**
  Someone may give examples of others who engage in fornication, friends, church members, family members, etc., and they are doing okay, but remember, every individual will stand before the Throne of God to give account. Nothing is hidden to Him. Don't compromise, and don't join the multitude to do evil.

> **Body Language:**
  Body language and attitude can reveal sinful intentions. There may be the demonstration of a person's intention through his or her body language. Just walk out of the scene as fast as your legs can carry you, when you perceive any contrary moves. Be strong in your resolve to resist the devil on this matter. Do not fall for the enticement to sin, your glory is at stake!

➤ **When You Don't Set Boundaries:**
A person that does not set boundaries on how to conduct themselves when visiting with the opposite sex easily falls into sin. For example, a lady walks into a guy's bedroom and innocently sits on the bed. That is an open invitation for immorality, even though it may not be your intention, because you did not think your action through. Men interpret things differently and so beware of how you behave around the opposite sex.

In whatever form or shape it comes, having self-control and determination to please God is highly essential. *"Resist the Devil...."* (Jas 4:7). You can overcome and protect yourself from falling into this kind of temptation by AVOIDING or limiting the following actions:

1. **Too much intimacy with your intended lady/man:**
It is advisable to reserve or keep your intimate closeness till your wedding day and thereafter. Unchecked or unrestraint intimate closeness could result in unconsciously falling into sin of immorality, especially if your emotional valve or gauge has never been tested. Because you

have not passed through this way before, do not put yourself on a dangerous emotional trip that it's outcome will cause you pain and shame.

2. **Passionate Touching**:
   You need to avoid touching each other's body inappropriately to avoid loss of self-control. Save that to when you get married.

3. **Late night visits**:
   It is advisable that intending couples limit the frequency of their visits to each other, especially late at night, to avoid the temptation of wanting to "**Relax and get some rest after a long day.**" Let the fear of God, who sees in secret, guide your relationship (Isaiah 29:15).

4. **Sleep over in each other's house:**
   Do not sleep over in each other's house for any reason. No matter the weather situation or transportation issue; find your way home. That is a trap to lure you into the sin of immorality. Even if you do not sleep over, avoid carelessly doing whatever you need to assist each other with in the bedroom. Ladies, take appropriate measures to protect your virtues. Do not let temptation snatch it from you and tear your

dress of many colors as we read in 2 Sam 13:11-12, 18-19

"And when she had brought them unto him to eat, he took hold of her, and said unto her, Come lie with me, my sister. And she answered him, Nay, my brother, do not force me; for no such thing ought to be done in Israel: do not thou this folly..... Howbeit he would not hearken unto her voice: but, being stronger than she, forced her, and lay with her.
And she had a garment of divers colours upon her: for with such robes were the king's daughters that were virgins apparelled. Then his servant brought her out, and bolted the door after her. And Tamar put ashes on her head, and rent her garment of divers colours that was on her, and laid her hand on her head, and went on crying."

5. **Long hours of visit**:
"Everything must be done in moderation...."
As much as possible, avoid spending long hours alone together; it's simply an invitation to lust. When you spend so much time together without people you are accountable to around you, boredom could set in, and strange ideas

would begin to flow in unintentionally. Before you know it, what began as an innocent visit may turn into a nightmare of regrets. Let's keep in mind the saying that **"Too much of anything is bad."** Therefore, intentionally plan your visits and make it as short as possible.

6. **Idleness**:
    "The Devil always finds work for idle hands." If all you do is sitting together and looking at each other's face during your visit, you are sending invitation to the devil to give you an assignment. Do also remember that all his assignments are deadly and devilish. He goes to and fro to see whom he will destroy. Don't give him a chance and don't allow him! Try to keep yourself busy by praying about your marriage and future, watching or listening to sermons, gospel music or home video. Playing motivational games like Scrabble, or Monopoly. In addition, make efforts to discuss topical issues of the scriptures, your careers, and plan your future prospects and family. These are few example of the ways of avoiding idleness.

7. **Excessive expression of love**:
Without disputing the fact that majority of the readers of this book are adults, yet, emphasis must be placed on limiting the excessive expression of your beauty and feelings toward each other. Don't give room or chance to uncontrollable emotion or inappropriate affection that may cause huge regrets. Keep the best part of the admiration and love expression of each other to the wedding day and everyday thereafter forever!

8. **Body Exposure:**
Never expose your body in an intimate way to each other, whether partially or completely. Being a Christian does not make you super human. Blood runs in your veins and you are an emotional warm blooded person. It is not the work of the Devil but a choice, if you let the other person fall because of you. Men are desperately moved by what they see, and if you, as a lady expose what is supposed to be covered it is simply called deliberate seduction. Avoid wearing straps, strapless, and backless dresses that leave little to imagination. When you are around each other, no flimsy night gowns or pajamas, reserve that until your honey moon night. Don't give room to

something that will be a stumbling block to your life and relationship. That Adam and Eve *"..were both naked and were not ashamed...."* (Genesis 2:25) began when God joined them together. Let yours also begin from your wedding day for ever. Wait for it patiently!

9. **Living together***:*
    Completely avoid living together under the same roof with your partner before marriage. It is a trap to sinful practices. The appropriate time to live together is after you are joined together in marriage. Be patient.

If your fiancé is in the habit of trying to lure you into sleeping with him through any of the points mentioned above or by other means not mentioned, know that the relationship is not going towards the right direction of a happy marriage instituted by God. It's rather for selfish satisfaction against the will of God. Pray for direction.

Threats of quitting the relationship must not lead you to compromise and do what may have a big negative impact on your life. Keep your body pure and holy. It is very honorable to remain a virgin till your wedding day. There is a saying among young ladies that **"Only fools and uncivilized ladies keep**

their virginity." Don't be deceived, men of valor still honor women of virtues. Not keeping your virginity is an erroneous belief, but if you still have yours at the time of reading this book, *PLEASE KEEP IT!*. If you happen to have lost yours at this point, pray for God's mercy and begin to keep yourself pure from now on. So many people were deceived and they fell into the pit of untimely loss of virginity, because of such statement above in order to fit into the society and prove to friends their upgraded level of civilization. Be grateful to God, for the opportunity to know the truth that many did not know before ignorantly making a great mistake.

Don't believe the lie that you cannot easily have a life partner who is a virgin, if you choose to keep yours, or that you may not have a partner at all, or that you will be seen as being too local and uncivilized to get married to. Don't fall victim to the lie of the devil. It is very wrong to promote the untenable lie of darkness. This is a distraction to make you compromise and bring you down. When you follow the truth the reverse will be the case; you will be honored and respected, and the one that God has assigned to you will surely come your way.

Contraceptive is a bad option when you are not married. Choosing to do this as a single lady is an admission that you have chosen to have preventive sex whenever the opportunity comes. It is very wrong to fulfill sexual desire before marriage by preventing pregnancy with family planning pills and procedure. **Remember, *it is called family planning, not singles planning.***

Preventive measure for men is not acceptable either for sleeping around with ladies with assurance of preventing pregnancy. Only husband and wife are approved by God to have sex. People call it unwanted pregnancy; that is very wrong, because you invited the pregnancy by sleeping around with somebody. The only approved preventive measure is abstinence or staying away from sex before marriage. Abortion can bring complete damage to the womb; and can claim your life. Both the baby and mother's lives are in danger, it is better to avoid this by controlling yourself and saying; "No" to inappropriate sexual activities.

Sometime ago, I watched a young lady share the story of her life on national television. At an early age of about nine, she was already singing praise and worship powerfully in the church choir. She later progressed to singing in front of over twelve thousand people in gospel concerts. Her gift was making room for her. In the process, while as a teenager, she miraculously got a good music recording contract. Unfortunately for her, she gave in to wrong association and relationship which led her to engage in pre-marital sexual intercourse, and she became pregnant for her deceitful boyfriend.

When she told him of her pregnancy, the boyfriend left her, and she was abandoned to her calamity. She never set her eyes on him ever again. Shamefully, she was in disgrace taken off the record contract with immediate effect. Her dream, career and ambition became shattered and ruined. She lost the opportunity to fulfill the plan and purpose of God over her life. ***There are some opportunities that come only once. You can jump over the huddles successfully if you discipline yourself and maintain your integrity***. Move closer to God and allow His Spirit to guide you.

Joseph refused to sleep with Potiphar's wife. He said "No" several times. He suffered for it for a while, but he finally got to His glorious destiny. You too can overcome temptation like Joseph (Genesis 39:7-9, 10 -21).

In one of my missionary journeys to a certain area in Jamaica, I met with some young ladies, between the ages of seventeen (17) and twenty-one (21) years old. While counseling with them, I discovered that eighty percent (80%) of them boldly and with enthusiasm, said that they tried not to get pregnant by using family planning method. They were speaking as if it was the right and normal thing to do. No, it's very wrong! Sex is only approved by God for husband and wife, starting from the wedding day.

Some ladies initiate sex too by pretending to be sick in order to create an atmosphere for touch, and then from that point one thing would lead to another. Remember that there are some ladies sent on a mission to defile the standing and devoted brothers "...*wherefore let him that think he is standing take heed less he fall*." - (1 Corinthians 10:12).

After all, it was Potiphar's wife that initiated the sex drive, and tried by all means through action, speech, look and touch, to make Joseph fall into temptation. But Joseph determined not to sin against God, and did everything to please Him. Pleasing God is a powerful key to overcoming temptation – *"... Should I sin against my God?"* (Genesis 39: 9).

Ask for discerning spirit, be a Bible scholar, and pray in the Holy Spirit. Be strong in the Lord, and don't fall into temptation. Respect yourself and bring honor to your body. Wait till you both say "**I do**" at the altar before sleeping together. Always, remember, sex was created by God for the enjoyment of HUSBAND AND WIFE, and also for procreation and not for anyone that is not married, regardless of their age.

CHAPTER 5
Parents And Spiritual Leaders Role/Mentorship

Understand Parents' And Spiritual Leaders Role. In choosing the right life partner, the roles of parents, pastors and spiritual leaders are very significant. The Bible encourages us in Ephesians 6:1-3 (NIV):

"Children obey your parents in the Lord, for this is right. "Honor your father and mother." - which is the first commandment with a promise - "so that it may go well with you and that you may enjoy long life on the earth." (Ephesians 6:1-3 (NIV))

It is very important to honor your father and mother's opinion in making a life decision in marriage. I mean, in this respect, both your biological, guardian and spiritual parents. These ones have gained ample life experiences, and hence they can pray, see far, make inquiry, and see the side that the young ones that are enveloped in love and inexperience cannot see.

Their prayer of intercession can bring divine insight and revelation that will open up every hidden thing about the relationship. Their appropriate intervention can reveal the true nature and intention of a partner. The best and lasting marriages are the ones with the support of parents.

Abraham prayed and told his servant to go to a particular tribe to get a wife for his son; the servant prayed and asked for a sign in order to choose the right lady. God approved Rebecca with signs and wonders in line with the prayer, and Isaac had a wonderful marital life with no threat of divorce. Obeying parents in the Lord is very right according to the Bible. It is the duty of the parents to pray, and pray through with divine revelation before approving the relationship, because they are accountable to God. Even though the children came to the world through them, yet it should be noted that

"..*Children are an heritage of the Lord..*" Psalm 127:3.

They are God's treasure gift to their parents. So many obedient and Bible based Christians listen and obey their parents. They rely on and believe their parents' information and opinion as true and right. This is why parents should be sure that they give right and God-inspired advice to their children. Though in some cases, children turn deaf ears to the parents' counsel. The consequences are always terrible.

Samson disobeyed his parents and had relationship with a lady from the land of the Philistines; he was betrayed and got defeated by the enemies through his wife Delilah that he married without the consent of his parents. A powerful and highly respected man of war died a shameful death in the hands of the Philistines (Judges 16: 3-21).

There are so many examples of couples in the Bible and in our generation that made it to the end, because of their parents' involvement. As it is for men, same also for women, both parties need to allow Godly parents' involvement. More honor, respect and dignity will be given to a lady who allows her parents' involvement spiritually and physically in her relationship. She will be treated better than someone proving to her partner that the Parents' opinions are not relevant in her relationship. Those who despise their parents' opinion and deny their involvement are most likely to fall into the pit of deceit, end up in wrong partners' arms and suffer a life time mistake. Such people are stuck with the spouse after marriage suffering in silence in deep sorrow, pain, and regret. They will find it too shameful to go back to their parents to tell them their experience since they despised and disobeyed their counsel because of someone that just crept into their lives. The moment your partner realizes that you don't have the backing of your family members, you are on your own and will be treated anyhow.

Remember, the position of parents is ever constant and the love is unconditional. No matter what happens to you, your parents can never forsake or abandon you. Separation or divorce is not possible between you and your parents. They are always there for you as long as they live. Listen to their godly counsel concerning your choice of life partner. Parental approval must be based on God's approval. It must be with pure mind with thorough inquiry of his or her family background. By experience the observation of a person's character, attitude and behavior can be easily perceived by parents. *The eyes of your parents are open when your eyes are closed in deep love.*

However, with great appeal to parents, please don't force your children to choose a life partner because of wealth, popularity, tribe, fame, etc., rather, pray and allow God to intervene and give you divine and clear revelation about it. With great passion, I want to appeal to parents, that you should not allow your children to marry anybody because of your past or current relationship with their parents or family members. Your good friend in the past may have changed to be a different person in character and life style today. Please don't impose a particular person on them. Don't do it for business partnership, politics, titles or any personal interests. Use your position wisely to guide them. Let God take control. But don't hesitate to alert them of any danger, through diligent search and as the Lord reveals.

There is a very low percentage rate of divorce in China, because parents play active role in the choice of their children's life partner. They honor and listen to their parents' opinion before they choose, and the final choice of life partner to marry is based on their parents' approval.

Spiritual leaders, e.g., God fathers or mothers, and Pastors, must be duly informed before any decision is made. Counseling and prayers are very important. Divine revelation, observation and also information from counseling are the key point for right decision. Their opinion must be in line with the parents' opinion. God is not an author of confusion. The Spirit of God will surely bear witness. Spiritual leaders can easily find out and tell much about the spiritual background of the partner, either in their church or another, while the parents can find out about the family background and character.

There cannot be a hiding place for a deceiver who plans to do "hit and run" in order to tamper with someone's spiritual life or destiny, through fake marriage proposal. With the involvement of biological and spiritual parents, surely such an evil intention or act will be exposed and truth will prevail. It is very dangerous to have a wedding done without the consent and approval of a minister of God. If the spiritual authority tells you to hold on concerning the marriage for a period of time, please do so. Don't go secretly to another church or place to marry out of rebellion, because your pastor instructed you to wait for a while. It is better to exercise patience for a period of time than to run into a great mistake.

"...*Obedience is better than sacrifice....*" (1 Samuel 15:22)

Thanks be to God for His ministers. For the wonderful work (which is the most delicate work on earth), especially in the area of counseling the singles before making a life choice of marriage partners. May the fresh anointing of God continue to flow in greater dimension upon you, in Jesus name. Keep doing what God has called you to do and not yielding to the voice of men in compromise. As we know, we are accountable to God concerning the people He has put under our care.

Beware and be careful about conviction based on fake dreams from intending couples, and other unacceptable reasons of a person they have in mind to marry at all cost. God's divine intervention should be looked into with clear proof before final approval. Regardless of his or her position, role, title, contribution and duration of membership, the truth must prevail. **Marriage is a life decision. Missing it may be missing God's divine plan and purpose**; and it is very fragile. Intending partners should depend on their pastors' opinion, and it is also alright for them to stand and maintain their grounds on the will and the word of God without fear or compromise.

There was a situation where a sister that had been waiting for a couple of years for a life partner, went to her Pastor with strong points and assurance of converting the man from his religion to Christianity. The man even followed her to church a few times. This sister was a fervent child of God and a devoted worker in her church, respected and loved. Unfortunately, her pastor approved the relationship of less than three months, with an unbeliever that claimed to have been converted to Christianity. The approval was granted because of the pressure from the lady, and his consideration for her many years of being single and conviction based on the man's promises. There was not enough time for counseling, and everything was in a rush and out of order.

Finally, the marriage was done in the lady's church. Few days after the wedding, her husband stopped her from praying, and he instructed her to take the Bible out of the house. The husband proved to her that his own religion was actively in effect and that he's not a Christian and was never one. Even though he had earlier on in their short courtship assured her to have been totally converted to Christianity before the wedding and promised to continue. The marriage ended up within a short time in a couple of months with a great and deep sorrow, coupled with regret on the part of this fervent and beautiful sister.

The sister was not patient enough to know who she was marrying because of inadequate time of courtship. she was deceived. Yet the duty of her pastor was to counsel them thoroughly and pray.

The minister had the authority to stop them and postpone the wedding ceremony, to allow for more time for the couple to know each other well while he sought the face of God. In some cases, the desperate individual makes it a "do or die" issue.

A life decision issue is too delicate to handle anyhow. It must be handled carefully. The relationship would have been discontinued and the wedding postponed based on the word of God that says:

"Do not be unequally yoked with unbeliever..." - (2nd Corinthians 6: 14-17).

It is better to break engagement than a marriage. Speaking the truth in love can save a lot of our singles from falling into wrong choices of life partners. The scriptures cannot be broken.

CHAPTER 6
Delay Is Not Denial

Since it is the will of God to be married, believe that there is a particular person assigned to be your chosen partner on this planet earth, and that is the one that you will eventually get married to. The question is, who is this person, and when is he or she going to show up? It doesn't matter if it happens early or late, the most important fact is that he or she will surely come. Know with assurance that there is somebody that you will be divinely connected with. You just need to wait patiently.

Don't rush into choosing a partner because of your age or status and end up with a wrong choice that will lead you to a terrible marriage which will be short lived. Getting married to the wrong person is the beginning of a miserable life and failure in fulfillment of destiny. Therefore be patient. Lady, there is a man looking for you; allow him to find you.

When a man chooses the wrong woman in haste as life partner and eventually marries her, it results in multiple life problems for many people! It becomes a chain reaction of terrible mistakes in marriage. It means that: the right man for the woman will marry a wrong person, when the one that God originally planned for him has married another man. The woman that he wrongly marries will also miss her own God-ordained husband. The circle of wrong partnership continues. This is one of the major causes of increase in the rate of separation, broken homes, violence, abuse, and divorce.

The fact that you are not yet married at your own calculated time does not mean that God has denied or forgotten about you.

"Can a woman forget her suckling child, that she should not she should not have compassion on the son of her womb? Yea they may forget, yet I will not forget you"- Isaiah 49: 15.

In most cases, God is preparing you for the best, and He is arranging the right partner for you. Mind you, God is the only one that can arrange the perfect one for you. Trust in the Lord and wait patiently. Yours is somewhere looking for you; let him find you. It's going to be through divine connection. Be encouraged and be in expectation. Keep hope alive and rejoice, he will surely come.

To you it may seem like delay, but in God's agenda, there is no delay at all. He is working on your situation, and He will make it happen in His time, which is the perfect time. God's time is the best.

*"**He has made everything beautiful in His time...**"*– (Ecclesiastes 3:11).

There is a waiting period for the best, lasting and successful marriage. *"**Though it may tarry, wait for it.**"* There are some reasons that can make you think and believe that you have a major issue of delay. These are:

1) **Pressures from friends** - Series of questions from engaged close friends concerning your marital status. Witnessing and discussing about your friends' marital life that reminds you of your own "still waiting" level.

2) **Family members** - Hearing comments from family members and getting disturbed with questions of "When is it going to happen?"

3) **Self condemnation** - Accepting the feelings of being too late because of age, mistakes, inferiority complex, anxiety, disappointments

and peoples' negative comments that the person's marital dream is never going to be fulfilled.

4) **Not working in God's vineyard** - When you're not spiritually engaged, and serve God in full capacity, it is easy for the devil to lie to you and mislead you. Serving in His vineyard is a weapon that sharpens your sensitivity so that you cannot be deceived by the anxiety inspired by the thoughts of suffering delay.

5) **Waxing cold** - The tendency to wax cold is very high, when one's desires or expectations are not being met at the expected time. Yet, ironically that is the time to pray more and be closer to God, with the hope and assurance that all shall soon be well as long as you are in the boat with Jesus.

6) **Not fervent in Christian life** - when a person's life is run without looking unto Jesus and author and finisher of His faith, he or she falls into the trap of being lukewarm and in despair. We are encouraged to be fervent in spirit; serving the Lord (Rom 12:11).

7) **Listening to wrong advice -** When you listen to people's opinion about your personal life, the desire to wait for God's time will be killed. The world is full of evil counselors who have their own personal agenda to fulfill outside of yours - so beware and wait patiently God is never late!

8) **Getting confused and anxious -** The forerunner to confusion is anxiety but God is not the author of confusion. When a person does not trust the Lord anxiety borne out of fear would creep in so that confusion could finish the job of destruction.

No matter your situation or condition, don't rush as a result of some or all the reasons listed above in order not to become tied to people you don't really know much about. Wait, relax and keep your hope alive in Christ Jesus! As a single Christian lady, wait, and keep serving God faithfully; you will eventually meet the perfect person for your life in the line of duty. You don't need to be looking and searching for a lost coin, but trust in the Lord and believe Him for the best. *It is better to marry late than to rush in and rush out.*

The problem of most divorced couples today is rushing into relationship because of their age, and long period of waiting. When you realize that you are at that age of choosing a life partner, it is very important to trust God, stay cool and calm and be patient. As you wait with the realization and full understanding that you don't own yourself, be sensitive to the leading of the Spirit of God. His thought and plan for you are good, to take you to your destination. Fulfilling the goal of your marital life is included in the package of your destiny.

Another salient observation is that some ladies try to do a lot of unnecessary things such as making strenuous efforts to get men attracted to them. In some cases, they actually succeed in seducing people and cause them to fall into the wrong hands, which eventually might end in regret. You just need to be original, be yourself and relax for God's chosen one will surely come your way. As long as you're doing the right thing at the right time according to the will of God, you can never miss the bone of your bone and flesh of your flesh, divine connection will be your testimony.

The way you dress is another thing to note of. Exposing your body, dressing nude, sagging, excessive make up, piercing of nose, tongue, and lips and having tattoos on your body are not things that would attract a sensible partner to you. It would in actual fact drive them far away from you. In addition, struggling to purchase very expensive dresses and shoes, painting your hair with different colors are not the hallmarks of a Godly woman. Ladies, your focus should not be outward adorning of clothes but of the inner beauty that reveals your Godly character as we read in 1 Peter 3:3-4:

"Whose adorning let it not be that outward adorning of plaiting the hair, and of wearing of gold, or of putting on of apparel; But let it be the hidden man of the heart, in that which is not corruptible, even the ornament of a meek and quiet spirit, which is in the sight of God of great price."

Please, *"Let all things be in moderation...."* You just need to dress up neatly and nicely, and honoring yourself by covering your body appropriately because *"Your body is the temple of God."*
Body exposure makes you look cheap, and lose respect. It's like a precious gift without a gift wrap. No decent man will be interested in a lady that is half naked. If you dress the way that is described earlier you will only attract irresponsible people that will 'pick and drop' you. There is a saying

that: "**Birds of the same feather flock together.**" Honorable men will be interested in women of integrity. Abnormal makeup and outrageous appearance can prevent your right partner from coming to you. It can send the right person away from your life, even though he is having the impression that you may be the right partner.

Be proud of your color. Bleaching to change your skin color is not a good option. God has given you the best skin color that fits you, and that is the one you are supposed to cherish. One of the greatest African leaders and philosopher, Dr. James Emmanuel Kwegyir Aggrey says: "**I am proud of my color; whoever is not proud of his color is not fit to live.**" Be careful about what you do to your body!

Some people get it wrong and make themselves look ten years older than their age in the name of Christianity. Wearing oversized, dirty, rough and old fashioned dresses, are the wrong steps to finding a life partner. Ladies, you need to take good care of your hair, wash it and fix it regularly; and allow fresh air into it so that it would not ooze with odor. You don't need to tie your hair for several months because it's untidy and claim you're keeping it so for religious purpose. Our God is a clean God, and He abhors unkempt look.

Taking your bath with non bleaching soap with good smelling gentle lotion is healthy for your body. You can also wear gentle deodorant and perfume in moderation. All round personal hygiene is necessary. However, beware of idolizing yourself and spending long hours in front of the mirror, in the name of making up. It is unacceptable excuse for you to go late to fellowship or work because of makeup. Let it be in moderation be a good time manager and spend it wisely.

While expecting your God-given life partner, set for yourself a goal of improving your life by choosing: career, education, vocation, ministry, apprenticeship etc.; and be on a ladder for future reliability. Settle down for one that you know you are strong enough to achieve, and add value to your life, so that you would not enter your marital life disadvantaged. ***Don't make yourself a present and future liability***. While praying and expecting, know that your career will activate and bring resounding confirmation to your partner. A man may think twice before approaching a lady that dropped out of high school deliberately while he just worked hard to earn his second degree from a good University. This may cause doubt and uncertainty for the man, and it may result in serious delay in his choosing you as a reliable partner, or worse still you may even miss the right person entirely. Don't be a lazy person as it may be a negative factor for timely connection to your life partner.

Be very committed to God's work. Be occupied with service in and outside the church and be a faithful and committed worker in His vineyard. Stay focused on Jesus Christ, "*the author and the finisher of your faith*." As you stay in your place of service, the right one will come.

Be careful and mindful of the friends you hang out with. You may end up being influenced by the kind of life your friends are living. Move with decent people that love the Lord and can positively influence your life.

"Be not deceived: evil communication corrupts good manners." (1 Corinthians 15:33)

You are known by the company you keep. You may not be easily reached by the right partner for your life if you remain in the company of indecent people.

Your character and attitude at home, school, work, church and in the public really matters; people are watching you. A man that beats up his mother will eventually turn his wife to a punching bag. A lady that quarrels with people in the church parking lot will eventually turn the husband's house to hell on earth; and peace will be far from that kind of home.

*"**Better to live in a dessert than to live with a quarrelsome and nagging wife.**"* Proverbs 21:19 (NIV))

The honor you give to your parents and ministers of God will prove your character to the person that is having the leading to ask for your hand in marriage. Don't let your character be a stumbling block to your God-ordained spouse. Esther, an orphan, obeyed her uncle Mordecai, the only one she knew as parent who brought her up and she honored him. Esther agreed to go to the palace for beauty context without question when Mordecai told her do so. That character reflected as she followed the instructions of Hegai (the custodian of the women in the king's palace in Shushan). She also obeyed in keeping her identity as instructed by her Uncle Mordecai. No wonder, she was chosen as the queen among all the ladies from twenty-seven provinces in a foreign land. (Esther 2:17).

We cannot overlook the fact that some people experience delay in having life partner due to attack of the enemy. This may be categorized into various ways: demonic attack from forces of darkness, generational curses, negative spoken words by someone, family circle pattern, evil covenant or spirit husband or wife operation. This is true and real. If you are having love affairs in your dream, having wedding ceremony, seeing yourself pregnant, breast feeding a baby, living with children and a spouse etc. You need to quickly go to your spiritual leader and cry out for deliverance so that the yokes can be broken by the anointing of the Holy Spirit in Jesus name.

"For we are not fighting against blood and flesh enemies, but against evil rulers and authorities of the unseen world, and against evil spirits of the heavenly places." (Ephesians 6:12 (NLT).

Thanks be to God for the victory available for us through the power in the name of Jesus.

" …. God also hath highly exalted Him and given him a name which is above every name: that at the name of Jesus every knee should bow, of things in heaven, and things in earth, and things under the earth; And that every tongue should confess that Jesus Christ is Lord……" (Philippians 2: 9-11)

You should be ready and available to be set free, so you can fulfill the plan and purpose of God for your life. You need to cooperate with God by surrendering yourself for victory. You have to be in unity of the spirit with the minister of God for total deliverance. It is necessary to keep, maintain or sustain your deliverance with fervent prayer and reading of the bible on daily basis. Most importantly seek to receive the Holy Ghost baptism, that you may speak in an unknown tongue as the Spirit of God gives you utterance. The above are important weapons required to resist the devil because he will make serious and fortified attempt to return as we read in Matthew 12:43-45

"When an evil Spirit leaves a person, it goes into the desert, seeking rest, but finding none. Then it sat I will return to the person I came from. So it returns and find former place empty, swept and in order. Then the Spirit finds seven other spirits more evil than itself, and they all enter the person and live there. And so that the person is worse off than before…." .

You need to be in a living bible based church that believes in the word of God and the power of the Holy Spirit because " ……*thou shall receive power*

after that he Holy ghost is come upon you......"
Acts 1:8

Please note that in so many cases, apart from the points mentioned previously, delay may be due to some other factors such as careless life style and ungodly attitude. Another reason may be as a result of keeping a memory of the bad experience of parents or family members' who went through unhappy and hateful marriage. Being a witness of a close friend's unsuccessful and short lived marriage. Suffering violently in silence with regret about other people's marital woes is an attack of the devil to make you lose interest in marital life. Do not carry the load that does not belong to you, by always see yourself and portion as different from them. Their cases may be due to wrong choice of life partner. That is the focus of this book, and it is written to guide you and keep you standing where others have fallen, so you have a better opportunity. You cannot remain single or lose interest in the opposite sex because of those experiences. Your decision should be based on the will of God that instituted marriage. As long as you do His will and follow the right guidelines, you will have a successful marriage with the right person.

Waiting time is a good period to keep yourself pure and holy to the Lord. Do not lose your dignity. Giving your body for ungodly practices is a bad option, it may cause long time or permanent delay that can defile you. Be a good bible scholar, prayerful, and attend fellowship regularly. It is very important to witness Jesus Christ to people more at this period because you are not yet committed to family obligations, children issues, etc. Make good use of this life opportunity to the glory of God. Have good and positive attitude. Be expectant and patiently wait for your glorious God given life partner. There is a perfect one for you and very soon there will be a divine connection at the right and perfect time.

Looking closely and considering the effect and result of choosing a life partner, it is clear that the major cause of problem in the world today is choosing a wrong life partner for marriage. The consequences are very great. It is a lifelong issue. and so it is worth carefully and patiently waiting for.

CHAPTER 7
Courtship

This is the most important and final part of the process of choosing a life partner. The final level of decision making for a lifelong journey, and a level in which final conclusion of a strong relationship between a man and a woman is made. A stage of determination and confirmation of the end product of the relationship. It is the period of getting the final approval from the Lord before the total submission to His will.

Courtship is the foundation upon which marriage is built, and it is its bedrock. The success and longevity of a marriage depends on the status or viability and strength of the courtship. It is the period of transition from single to married life, and it is like an elevator that takes you to the final destination of marriage. It is a bridge that leads to marital life, and it is a good time to discuss about the real picture of life after your wedding. It is this period you express and share views about very vital issues in your intending new home.

There are so many factors and guidelines that can help to determine the approval of a courtship for successful graduation to marriage:

1. Prayer

Prayer is very important to sustain and keep the courtship strong and pure. It keeps the spiritual antenna sensitive, and suppresses the flesh in subjection to the Spirit of God. Prayer keeps you in tune with God and enables you to get divine direction and instructions. This includes regular personal prayer, joint prayer with partner, group prayer with brethren, prayer with parents and spiritual leaders. You can never make a mistake or fall if you are engaged in fervent prayer as the word of God says "***Pray without ceasing.***" (1 Thessalonians 5:17).

That is the key and the weapon to reveal deep and invisible things that are ahead in the relationship. Prayer during courtship will bring confirmation concerning the relationship by divine revelation. It is a very sensitive time to listen attentively to the still small voice either to proceed, stop or give the waiting more time. Pray daily without ceasing and, don't be weary or tired at the verge of completing the race. Be fully covered by His armor, it is then that you can resist temptation.

"Put on the whole armor of God that you may be able to stand against the plans of the devil For we wrestle not against flesh and blood, but against principalities and powers, against the rulers of the darkness of this world...." (Ephesians :11-12)

2. Time for Courtship

There must be a quality time for courtship, and this is to enable you to really find out and know a lot about the person you want to spend the rest of your life with. There is no specific time for courtship since each individual case in relationship is unique. It depends on how long it takes you to collect all the necessary information and to discover the important aspects of his or her life that you need to know, most especially, the time that you receive confirmation from the Lord in any way He chooses to confirm it to you.

The suggested duration is approximately twelve to eighteen months. Courtship that is too short may not totally reveal who your partner is. A courtship that is too long can cause temptation that may lead to regret and end up in complete separation. Do not rush, and don't stay in courtship forever either. Do it in moderation.

3. Influence of Intimacy during Courtship

Do everything in your power to make sure that inappropriate or excessive intimacy that not ruin your courtship. No matter how spiritual you are, because you are a human being, you respond to touch, sight and the auditory stimuli. So when you begin to touch each other amorously, at first innocently without evil intention, say emotionally arousing words and exposing sensitive parts of your bodies to each other, then you are starting a fire that the most accomplished fire fighter in the world cannot put off. It would only take the intervention of heaven to stop you on that emotionally damaging road trip.

Beloved, it is very wrong to sleep together during courtship. You must respect each other's body and keep it pure until the wedding day. Avoid being together alone in the bedroom, and stop unnecessary night visits that can reasonably lead to a sleep over - so be careful. Short visits during the day should be preferable, but let it be in moderation. My suggestion is three times in a week at the most, and with those you are accountable to within earshot. Even phone calls should not be excessively made, maybe once a day should be alright, except for important and special reasons. He or she may be tired of your frequent calls, and there is a saying that, *"Too much familiarity breeds contempt."* Therefore, save your frequent phone calls to him or her till you get married.

4. **Do not Cohabitate during Courtship**

Do not move in with your partner during courtship. It is immoral, and it is a violation of God's plan for marriage. It is a stolen level of intimacy that would undermine your relationship. According to research, it has about fifty percent (50%) chance of causing unstable marriage or even end in divorce. Respect precedes love; build it up. Don't depend on one another to satisfy emotional desires, it devalues your esteem, therefore exercise self-control.

Decide what your limit will be and courteously maintain it. Be conscious of your partner's mood when you are together and let him or her go as soon as you notice weakness in each other's emotion. Don't compromise by convincing yourself that at least we would soon get married, so it's okay. No! It is not, the Bible calls it fornication. Also do not take advantage of your partner's weakness especially if you're the stronger one., but let the fear of God step in as you exercise self restraint.

It is against the will of God to have sex before marriage. If you have fallen victim in this regard, ask for God's mercy and forgiveness, as you read this book. He will surely forgive you, only don't do it again until your wedding day because " *...If we confess our sins, he is faithful and just to forgive us our sins and cleanse us from all unrighteousness.*" - (1 John 1:9). God is merciful, and He is also a consuming fire. Don't take Him for granted by continuing in sin.

"For if we sin willfully after we have received the knowledge of the truth, there remains no sacrifice of the truth...It is a fearful thing to fall into the hand of the living God."- (Hebrews 10:26, 31).

Understand that God's intention for *sex is for enjoyment as a sacred gift for men and women after marriage*. It's only meant for married couples. It is also for procreation;

increase and multiplication is God's idea and plan for couples from the beginning of creation (Genesis 1:28).

Sexual intercourse should not be an activity that people in courtship should engage in. Human nature and flesh may bring about the request; do not give in. A partner that demands for sex persistently and makes it a criterion for marriage may not be your God-assigned partner. You need to pray more and request prayer from family and spiritual leader for confirmation. The relationship may be for satisfaction of sexual desire and not true love. Remember you are receiving a license for this on your wedding day, with heavenly approval that gives you freedom to do it as many times as you want either day or night. So relax and be patient.

As a Christian, It is glorious to remain a virgin till your wedding day. This is applicable to both male and female, though people often think it's only for ladies. For one reason or another, if you happen to have lost your virginity, call upon God for His mercy and glory to come upon you. He will give you a new start. People have lost their virginity in various ways contrary to their wish. It could be by force, deceit, ignorance, rape, fear of losing their partner, imitation, wrong information and so on. Some happen due to lack of self control, whatever the case may be God in heaven will give you a new start if you call upon Him. Passionate physical touch must not be used for satisfaction of personal or emotional need. Maturity and power of self-control must be displayed in respect and honor for each other at courtship level.

5. *Be guided by Love and not by Lust*
Self-control is part of the fruit of the Spirit. Stop any activity that may grieve the Holy Spirit, and don't put yourself in a situation that will mess with your emotion. Purity paves the way for intimacy, and the wait is worth it. Too bad and so sad that some relationships end tragically in courtship because of immorality. Some ladies lost their lives during abortion. Some are abandoned because of the pregnancy that occurred during courtship. No wonder there is increase in single parenthood. Some cover up using contraceptives. A lot of ladies lost their dignity and honor as a result of falling victim to the alluring vice of immorality, and which later resulted in shameful and painful separation before wedding. No wonder a lot of marriages come to tragic end within

the early months of wedding. It is very important that you maintain a high standard, keeping in mind that you are spending the rest of your life with him or her. Don't settle for less or mediocre relationship, when God has something exceptional for you. Don't eat hot soup in a hurry, or else you may end up burning your tongue!

"*Flee fornication. Every sin that a man does is outside the body, but he who commits sexual immorality sins against his body*." (1 Corinthians 6:18)

Meeting in the right and appropriate place at the right time is a great opportunity to avoid temptation during courtship. This is a very delicate and tempting stage where people are very anxious to come together. A lot of people have fallen at this level because of impatience. Some men make it a must to sleep with the ladies since they are both in agreement to marry anyway. Try your best to successfully jump over this huddle. Be patient. *When the lady says one three-letter word 'yes' to marry you, wait to complete the process with your own two-word statement, "I do," to get the license, approval and authority of heaven and earth to live, sleep and do everything together as husband and wife.*

6. Character

No one is perfect, and everybody has one flaw or another. You should be able to discover your partner's flaws during courtship, but make sure it is minor, that is, something you can handle for the rest of your life. If you think you will find it difficult to cope with such an issue, please don't put yourself in everlasting bondage. At the end, it will turn to "**Suffering in silence**" kind of situation. Closely observe and watch the character of your future spouse. Don't overlook dangerous warning sign such as disloyalty to authority, anger, disrespect, addictions, unfaithfulness, etc. Do a thorough research and deal with the issues and don't assume that the behavior or character would get better after marriage. Observe the tempo as the courtship progresses and *understand that you can never change him or her after marriage. Some people think that way. No! It will not happen. What is not completely dealt with during that period of courtship may never be done for ever*. Somebody that cheats once on you before marriage will probably cheat ten times more on you after the wedding.

Anger is a terrible thing. It's the worst and very difficult emotion to deal with. It's not easy to let go except through total surrendering to the power of the Holy Spirit.

"Make no friendship with an angry man..." - (Proverbs 22:24a).

"Be not hasty in thy spirit to be angry, for anger rests in the bosom of fools" - (Ecclesiastes 7:9).

Your partner must realize and admit the presence of anger in his life and be ready to let go. Help your partner with scriptures and prayers to deal with it. If it's not genuinely dealt with, find your way out of the relationship. This can cause a big problem and regret after the wedding. Please take this seriously. Do you know that your children may fall victim of chronic anger that may negatively affect their lives? A lot of marriages end in tragedy of murder, suicide and jail because of anger. Be wise.

If you are regularly being disrespected during courtship, expect double abuse and dishonor after marriage. You and your partner are supposed to genuinely complement each other. If your partner happens to slap or beat you during courtship, be ready to become a punching bag in your marital life. Don't see his or her abuse of your person as a mistake; it's just an example of what you will face for life. Respect and honor is very important; the way this is handled during courtship will determine and show a true picture of your experience after marriage and forever. Deal with it or quit now while it is yet redeemable.

Your observations about your partner's relationship with other people must be seriously taken note of. Pretence may come into play concerning his or her attitude towards you because of his or her desire. Watch out!

Find out genuinely and be sure of whom you are going to make a life covenant with. A BROKEN COUTRSHIP IS BETTER THAN A BROKEN MARRIAGE.

Make sure you do the following by checking and confirming if he or she is really:

- Kind and compassionate
- Have self-control, integrity, forgiving and letting go spirit
- Faithful in little or major things
- Gentle tongue (in speech, utterance)

- Admitting that he or she is wrong when wrong, and taking responsibility for his or her actions.
- Humble and meek

7. **Spiritual Life:**
   Courtship is the best time to really go deep into the spiritual background of your partner. You need to find out and confirm if he or she is a genuine Christian. It is very vital that you find out about your partner's prayer life. Seek to know the level of his or her knowledge and understanding of scriptures and Christianity. At least, within one year of relationship, you should be able to find out the facts. Do so before you go into deeper commitment with each other.

   Try to know the choice of words, the language used in emergency or stressful situations. The expression and action used to describe good or bad situations when they happen unexpectedly.

8. **Jokes and Compliments:**
   Be on your guard to find out if his or her jokes and compliments are positive, and if they are in tune with Christian motives or just common worldly expressions with inappropriate words.

For example, when something good happens and your partner says, "I thank the stars" or, "You are lucky" instead of giving thanks to God and call it a blessing from God or acknowledge it as a miracle. Be careful with such people.

"A good man out of the good treasure of his heart brings forth that which is good; and an evil man out his evil treasure brings forth that which is evil; for of the abundance of the heart his mouth speaks" - (Luke 6:45)

Partners who speak foul language are virtually empty on the inside, and when speaking they draw out of the abundance of their hearts. They draw from what they have stored up in them. If you can not completely deal with it in courtship, know that it can only get worse after you get married. By their fruits you will know them. A man of the spirit speaks the word of truth and speaks with the wisdom of God.

Note that, It is not easy to live with a man or woman who is full of anger. The older they become the greater the anger level. A man or a lady that slaps and beats you up when there is a little argument and calls it a mistake, is likely going to make beating you up a daily routine after marriage. Screaming, unnecessary yelling during conversation, using unpleasant body language, hissing, violent rage, body vibrations due to uncontrollable anger, constant hot argument and so on are **warning signs of serious anger issues**. It can be a terrible mistake to marry an angry person who can easily destroy properties, life, relationships, family, reputation, job, business, etc. The Spirit of God cannot manifest in a home with argument, strife and quarrel. All these are developed from anger.

Children raised in such family are most likely to inherit the anger issue and pass it on to generations. It can be dealt with if the person with the issue is able to identify the problem and be ready to get out of it. This may include self-control, spiritual efforts; reading scriptures on anger, listening to sermons and saying prayers. Let it get to stable level and be sure it is thoroughly and completely over before surrendering your life to such person. You cannot do anything about it after the wedding. It will only get worse.

Prayer life and constant Bible study is a good way of determining the spiritual life of your partner. Who always initiates it, and what is his or her attitude towards the other person that initiates it? You and your partner must occupy yourselves with constant fervent prayer and Bible study to suppress the flesh during courtship. The stronger party should help the other in the process of spiritual growth.

Choose specific day of the week to fast and pray together. Guide your heart (Proverbs 4:23). Make sure that you don't turn the relationship to marathon fasting exercise. Do all things in moderation. Have time to watch appropriate movies and listen to inspirational music and messages together.

9. **Surprise Visit:**

Make unexpected visits to your partner once in a while during courtship. You need to know who he or she really is behind the scene. Meet him or her in the real self without previous preparation for your visit. It should not be the norm or every time though.

10. **Know the Parents**

Visit each other's parents, and wisely find out about their faith and lifestyle. Watch the relationship of your partner with his or her parents. The one that insults and disrespects his or her parents will definitely do much more to you. Give room for background check. Find out necessary information about him or her about relationship with parents from people that really knows with wisdom.

11. Observation

Be sure that it is really true and genuine love you are experiencing (1 Corinthians 13: 4-7). If you find out that it is not genuine love, ***Stop.*** *D*on't risk it. It's a life journey; do not let it end in perdition.

12. Examine your Personal Motive.

Make sure it's not to meet your own selfish end, but genuine affection. Wrong motive will result in collapse of the marriage within a short period, like a house built upon sinking sand.

13. Engagement Pattern Varies

As per Christian standard the best recommended time for engagement from both sides should be towards the completion of a successful courtship. By then you already know who you want to spend your life with. You are sure of what you are putting yourself into as a life commitment. Accepting or giving engagement ring to someone you don't really know and genuinely love is a very wrong and dangerous step.

14. The Food He Loves and Appreciates

During courtship, the woman should try to know the favorite foods of her partner and how to make them. Good food will touch the heart of your husband and make him happy. *"A hungry man is an angry man."* Some women have lost their husbands to other women because of the issue of food; either not cooking regularly or the food she cooks is bad. A starving husband will look for alternative way of getting food from somewhere or somebody else. Plan ahead after the marriage to keep your partner indoor and enjoy him to the fullest. The foundation is laid during courtship. Learn to satisfy your spouse with the kind of food that he likes during courtship. Watch his attitude towards food when he is hungry and when full. Does he appreciate your cooking with compliments, or does he despise your hard work of cooking? Find out and see if you are pleased with his remarks before the final "Yes."

15 Agree on the Number and Gender of Children

Discuss and be in agreement concerning the number of children and the gender that you want God to give to you. Discuss and be sure about the number of children you want to have. Many marriages fall apart because of disagreement concerning the issue of children they desire. Some even come up with the idea of not having children at all after their wedding. Some want fewer kids than others.

In addition during courtship come to an agreement that you will both appreciate God for the gender of the children He gives to you; also, that you will be grateful for God's will concerning child bearing in marriage. Don't start to blame, argue or fight each other after the wedding concerning the issue of children. You cannot create one.

Have a serious heart-to-heart talk about the issue of male and female children very well, and be very certain of his stand on the matter. This must be settled during courtship. Giving birth to only female children has caused so many marriages to crumble. A lot of women have been abandoned with their female children for that reason. Some still live together as cats and dogs, enduring the marriage instead of enjoying it. These are the days where even some men look out for women, outside of their marriage, who will carry male children for them because of pressures from home and friends.

To avoid this serious issue, you must sit down and discuss in details with your partner with a reasonable conclusion. Both of you must realize that God is the giver of all good gifts. You can pray together and ask for the type of children that you want and allow the will of God to prevail. Remember that children are a gift from God, regardless of the gender. **Understand that both male and female children are very important and glorious**. Hanna specially asked for a baby boy and God granted her request. He is the unquestionable God. He knows the best for you **but t**here must be agreement, don't be fooled!

"Can two work together except they agree?" (Amos 3:3)

16. Know the Strength and Weakness.

Do all you can to get to know the strength and the weak point of each other, the interest and displeasure, the do's and don'ts. Remember you are coming from different families. You may even be from different tribes or race. The individual differences should be taken into consideration, and a reasonable conclusion, with personal conviction should be reached from both sides before the final commitment.

17. Christian Counseling

There should be well organized Christian marriage counseling towards the end of a successful courtship. Preparation for marriage can begin after approval from the counseling. Parents and mentors in the Lord must be in agreement with you on both sides for the marriage. Arrangement should be made for both family members for formal introduction to know each other before the wedding ceremony.

It does not make sense to put yourself under unnecessary stress, anxiety, worries and struggling in order to have extravagant wedding ceremony. Some people have lost their God-given spouse because of raising fund for expensive marriage, stretching themselves beyond their financial capability. Do not allow disagreement and argument on flamboyant materials for the wedding to ruin your lives. Why should you begin your new life in debt?

Make your wedding preparation simple, moderate and affordable. Agreement with each other on moderate choices is a good sign for wonderful marriage. Let your mind be set on the holy joining with your God-given husband or wife to be, and not in the party and expensive attires. Don't extend your courtship because of extravagant wedding ceremony. Be wise. Marriages with debt bring deep rooted strife, quarrel and worries. You are supposed to live within the abundant blessing of your financial capability and enjoy your marriage.

Both of you should sit down and be in agreement amicably with the program and expenses considering your financial budget. Relying on gifts and friends' promises may lead to disappointment. Inviting large crowd beyond your budget is not necessary. "**Cut your coat according to your cloth.**" It's so sad that some good relationships turned into strife and hot argument at the stage of preparing for wedding. In some cases, arguments caused by financial frustration have led to total break up.

18. **The Real Person**

Make sure that you see the actual face and the hair of your partner before the final day. Don't allow yourself to be in serious shock on your honeymoon by the time the makeup is cleaned up and the wig removed, only to discover that you are seeing a completely different lady: that is, you are beholding the real color of the face, the original shape of the head, and the real standard of hair that you least expect. This may be the end of the beginning. Making corrections about your expectation can still be made before the 'D' day. Both of you should tell each other if there is any hidden unusual mark or deformities in your body, to avoid big surprise. For example, replacement or transplant in any part of your body, removable denture, tattoo, eyes condition, tribal marks on the chest and the stomach areas, which is common in some parts of Africa etc. Let your partner know about your medical fitness. It is advisable that both of you should go for complete physical checkup before the wedding.

Preparation For Marriage
The wisdom of God and a lot of patience should be carefully put to work when preparing for the "Big day" - the wedding ceremony. It could be stressful and overwhelming, so take it easy, allow peace and understanding to reign between you and your partner. Be in agreement and work things out amicably. Give assignments concerning the event to close friends and family members to handle as division of labor. Avoid stress.

Results of not handling preparatory period for marriage well are:

I.   Breaking up before the wedding day
II.   Divorce at the early part of marriage
III. Living in poverty and debt after wedding
IV.   Lack of love, peace, unity, affection and joy. The marriage is in bad shape.
V.   Suffering in silence
VI.   Argument, fights, regrets and frustration.

When the crowd is gone, it's now just the two of you. Be careful. Plan your budget well and give room for your personal and living expenses after the wedding. As much as possible avoid argument on the choice of venue, date, and clothes etc. Take it easy and handle it very well. Relax and understand that it is just a ceremony, the most important thing is to have peace, joy and sustain the existing genuine love between both of you before, during and after the wedding. Pray for God's grace to lead and direct you, always remember to call upon Him and He will take absolute control:

"Call upon me and I will answer you......" (Jeremiah 33:3A (NIV))

Take note: **What your partner can not stop doing before your marriage may never be stopped for ever**. No matter the promise or vow, if you cannot see genuine change in whatever the case may be, don't risk it. Don't jump to a river that you know will drown you. Be in unity. Have a discussion and reach a good conclusion. Courtship is the last bus stop and final stage of putting finishing touches to relationship before marriage. Handle it well. Make it pure and holy. Don't fall into last minute temptation of immorality a couple of days or weeks to your wadding. It may cause a serious damage to your relationship with your spouse and stain your long waiting purity before GOD. It may even end the relationship completely.

"Trust in the Lord with all your heart; do not lean in your own understanding, acknowledge him in all your ways and He will direct your path……"- (Proverbs 3: 5-6).

Your choice of life partner determines the pattern of your life and fulfillment of your destiny. The process begins right from the day the woman says, "YES," to the day the man says, "I DO." Take note that the person you choose to marry comes with full package of the past, present and future. The package automatically becomes the property of both of you. Watch out for the type of package you are going to be responsible for. Make a wise and Godly decision according to God's plan and will. Make a final choice wisely with genuine love.

WORDS OF TRUTH

Beloved, in order to have genuine love for others, you need to acknowledge that God loves you. God Himself is love.

> *".....God is love.....,"* (1 John 4:8)

This love was demonstrated by the assurance that whosoever believes in JESUS CHRIST shall not perish but have **everlasting life.** He is stretching the unconditional hands of love to you today. Regardless of the gravity of your sin.

"Come now and let us reason together, saith the Lord; though your sin may be as scarlet, they shall be as white as snow, though they be red like crimson, they shall be as wool..." - (Isaiah 1:18).

His desire is to forgive you completely, save you, transform your life to become His child, cause you to enjoy all the benefits of sonship and give you eternal life. Jesus Christ came to the world in form of man; to save us from the consequences of the sin committed by Adam and Eve. He was crucified and His innocent BLOOD was shed for the remission of our sins. He died on the cross, and rose on the third day. He is alive forever! The good news is that He is coming back again to take those that believe in Him to heaven, to a beautiful place that cannot be compared to the best place in this world - a place of everlasting peace and joy. Today is your day! Tomorrow may be too late, therefore confess your sins, forsake them, repent today and surrender your life totally to Jesus Christ as your Lord and Savior.

This world is a temporary place. Either you like it or not you will exit from it one day - it's just a matter of time. But the question is where will you go when you die? You can only choose your everlasting home now that you are still breathing, to be either heaven or hell.

"Repent therefore and be converted, that your sins may be blotted out, when the time of refreshing shall come from the presence of the Lord...." - (Acts 3:19)

Go to a Bible believing Church and get baptized, worship and serve the LORD.

"....Repent and be baptized every one of you, in the name of Jesus Christ for the forgiveness of your sin. And you will receive the gift of the Holy Spirit ..." (Acts 2:38 (NIV))

Jesus Christ is coming back again to judge the world. Only those that believe in Him will reign and rule with Him in heaven for ever. There are a lot of signs and fulfillment of prophecies confirming His coming. Nobody knows the exact time, but He will surely come at anytime very soon.

Those that reject the free gift of salvation through Him will end up in everlasting fire. He does not want anyone to perish, but have everlasting life. Accept His unconditional love. If you have been born again but you backslid, use this opportunity to get back on track with the Lord immediately. He will have mercy on you and create in you a new heart and renew a right Spirit within you. His arms are wide open to receive you. Prepare for His coming

PRAYER

LORD, I thank you for your love for me. Before I was formed in my mother's womb you knew me. Thank you for the unconditional love. Today I obtain your mercy that is leading me to abundant grace, to love you, serve you and totally surrender to your will and your ways. I ask and receive forgiveness for all my sins and grace to live a new life in you, full of your Holy Spirit.

I trust and depend on your grace and power to patiently make a wise choice of the right partner, that I will live with for the rest of my life. Let my steps be ordered by you. Be my guide and lead me according to your plan and purpose. I totally submit to your will and to your ways. I receive the ability to successfully choose my God-ordained life partner, in Jesus name. Amen.

About The Book

This book is a total package of the right way of choosing the person you want to live with for life. It is a guide to help you recognize the right partner and maintain healthy relationship from courtship up to marriage level and for life. From reading this book you will know what to do if you are still single. It will give you clear understanding of the relationship you are in right now if it's right or not. You will also realize the source of your broken relationship if you have or are experiencing one right now and solution to the situation.

Choosing a life Partner, is a very important decision in life. Whoever you choose to spend your life with will determine the success or failure of your destiny, career, ministry and entire life. *Your life rotates around the person you choose to be your spouse. Your choice can build or destroy you. It can make or mar your future. A life partner is someone you will be with for the rest of your life.*

Note that you are partaker of the full package of the past, present and future of whoever you choose to marry. Search your conscience and pray before choosing. Be sure that it's not driven by ulterior motive. *Life after marriage depends on the strength of a particular choice of partner, and your choice determines the stability and longevity of the marriage.*

This book is written to guide and prevent you from going through the wrong route, making the same mistakes and falling into the same pit like many others, due to ignorance and lack of necessary information. "Knowledge is power." Beyond any doubt, it is a fact that the major cause of problems in society today is *wrong choice of life partner.*

Are you tired of being single, jilted, separated? Are you confused about relationships? Are you living a life of loneliness? Have you faced constant betrayal and disappointment concerning a life partner? Are you caught up in relationship full of battle and violence? Are you about to give up on life partner issues? All these and more - whatever your case, you will find solution to your situations in this book.

ABOUT THE AUTHOR

Esther F. Akinladenu is an anointed minister of the word, operating in the five- fold ministry. She is the founder of the Great Commission Fulfillment Ministries Worldwide. She is called by God to preach the Gospel and raise more evangelists through discipleship and training. Pastor Esther is an ordained Pastor and Evangelist, who speaks in conferences, crusades, churches, healing, deliverance, youth, singles, women, prophetic and at miracle services.

Her evangelistic zeal delivered with the demonstration of God's power in her missionary journeys has led to the planting of churches around the world including USA and Africa. She is in partnership in the ministry with her husband, Pastor Ebenezer Akinladenu. They are blessed with glorious children

Made in the USA
Coppell, TX
07 January 2020

14186747R00069